My First Haggadah

It's the beginning of spring! Everything is growing, the wind is gently blowing. The trees are green once again, the birds flying above our heads. We can finally go outside and play in the sun!

The arrival of spring also means it's time to celebrate Passover. In Hebrew, the holiday is called Pesach.

We prepare our house for Pesach, and the whole family helps.

We clean the house and remove all the chametz from it. Chametz is bread and other kinds of food we don't eat during Pesach.

We prepare special food and all our favourite dishes for the Seder feast.

The holiday lasts for a whole week! We welcome it with the Seder. Seder means order. We follow an order during the meal. Before we eat, we read a special book called the Haggadah.

Haggadah means "telling". It has stories, songs and blessings that tell the story of how the Jewish people were freed from slavery in Egypt.

Long ago in Egypt, there was an evil king named Pharaoh. He made the Jewish people who lived there work very hard, building cities and palaces without rest or much food. They were tired and hungry.

The Pharaoh was especially evil to the Jewish children and wanted to get rid of them. Among them was a baby boy born to a brave mother called Jocheved. To protect her son, she hid him for as long as she could. But, when she could no longer hide him, she put him in a cradle and sent him floating down the river, where Pharaoh wouldn't find him.

When the Pharaoh's daughter, the princess of Egypt, came to bathe in the river, she saw the baby and decided rescue him and take him home.

The baby's clever sister, Miriam, saw the princess rescue her brother and approached her. She offered to find a person to care for the baby. The princess accepted and Miriam quickly brought her mother, Yocheved, whom the princess hired as a nurse. Yocheved was happy to be able to nurse and care for her son and teach him all about his people.

The princess named the baby Moses, which in Hebrew means "brought out of the water."

As Moses grew, he couldn't bear to witness the hardships faced by the Jewish people. He left the grand palaces of Egypt and became a shepherd in a faraway land.

While Moses was caring for his sheep, he saw a burning bush and heard a voice coming from it, revealing it was God. God asked Moses to go to Egypt and free the Jewish people from the evil Pharaoh.

Moses journeyed back to Egypt, standing before Pharaoh and pleading, "Let my people go!" But Pharaoh, with a heart as tough as stone, refused to listen.

God was angry with Pharaoh and punished him ten times. These punishments were called plagues. Each one was a powerful event.

First, the water turned bright red. Then, frogs started leaping everywhere. Bugs called lice and flies filled the air. The sky darkened during the day, animals became sick, and people got red bumps called boils.

A wild hailstorm followed, accompanied by the beating of drums.
Punishment after punishment, until finally, Pharaoh agreed to let the Jewish people go.

The Jewish people got ready to leave very quickly. They didn't have time to bake bread for their journey, so they carried raw dough on their backs. The sun turned it into crunchy crackers called matzah.

Led by Moses, they followed him to a big sea. God told Moses to lift his walking stick, and like magic, the sea parted. They walked through on dry land.

When they were finally safely out of Egypt, Moses led them in songs of thanks to God.

Of course, the Pharaoh did not let the Jewish people leave just like that and sent his army after them. But when the Jewish people reached the sea, with the Egyptian soldiers closing in on them, God told Moses to raise his staff and the sea split in half, and the Jewish people walked across. When the Egyptians followed, the sea closed on them.

And so we start the Seder,
remembering the journey of the Jewish people.

LIGHTING THE CANDLES

We welcome the holiday by blessing and lighting candles.
We thank God for the festival lights, and for bringing our
family and friends together to celebrate Pesach.

בָּרוּךְ אַתָּה יְיָ אֱלֹהֵינוּ מֶלֶךְ הָעוֹלָם, אֲשֶׁר קִדְּשָׁנוּ בְּמִצְוֹתָיו וְצִוָּנוּ לְהַדְלִיק נֵר
שֶׁל שַׁבָּת וְשֶׁל יוֹם טוֹב

*Baruch Atah Adonai Eloheinu Melech ha'olam asher
kid'shanu b'mitzvotav v'tzivanu l'hadlik ner shel Yom Tov.*

בָּרוּךְ אַתָּה יְיָ אֱלֹהֵינוּ מֶלֶךְ הָעוֹלָם, שֶׁהֶחֱיָנוּ וְקִיְּמָנוּ וְהִגִּיעָנוּ לַזְּמַן הַזֶּה
*Baruch Atah Adonai Eloheinu Melech ha'olam shehecheyanu
v'kiyemanu v'higianu lazman hazeh.*

RECITING THE KIDDUSH

The Seder begins with the kiddush – the blessing over a cup of wine. Wine stands for the sweetness and joy of a holiday celebration.

בָּרוּךְ אַתָּה יְיָ אֱלֹהֵינוּ מֶלֶךְ הָעוֹלָם בּוֹרֵא פְּרִי הַגָּפֶן.

Baruch Atah Adonai Eloheinu Melech ha'olam, borei p'ri hagafen.

Thank You, God, for the grapes that grow to make wine for our holiday celebration.

בָּרוּךְ אַתָּה יְיָ אֱלֹהֵינוּ מֶלֶךְ הָעוֹלָם, שֶׁהֶחֱיָנוּ וְקִיְּמָנוּ וְהִגִּיעָנוּ לַזְּמַן הַזֶּה.

Baruch Atah Adonai Eloheinu Melech ha'olam shehecheyanu v'kiyemanu v'higianu lazman hazeh.

Thank You, God, for bringing us together to celebrate Pesach.

THE SEDER TABLE

The Seder table is special – not like our usual supper. There are three matzah covered with a cloth, a bowl of saltwater, an extra cup of wine, and a big plate with special foods: a bone, an egg, bitter herbs, parsley and sweet charoset.

Why do we have all these things on the table? The Passover Seder is different from our regular meals.

Asking questions helps us learn. The Haggadah asks four questions.

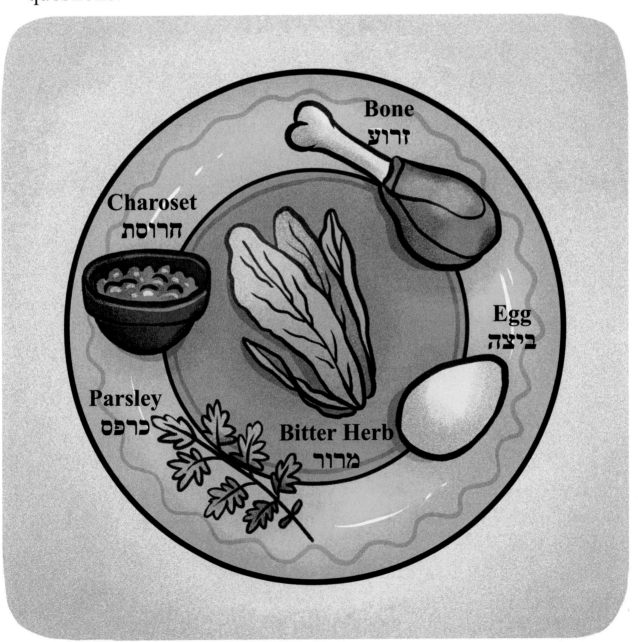

THE FOUR QUESTIONS

מַה נִּשְׁתַּנָה הַלַּיְלָה הַזֶּה מִכָּל הַלֵּילוֹת

Mah nishtanah halailah hazeh mikol haleilot.

Why is this night different from all the other nights?

1)

שֶׁבְּכָל הַלֵּילוֹת אָנוּ אוֹכְלִין חָמֵץ וּמַצָּה, הַלַּיְלָה הַזֶּה כֻּלּוֹ מַצָּה?

Sheb'chol haleilot anu ochlin chametz u'matzah. Halailah hazeh kulo matzah.

On all other nights we eat all kinds of bread. Why do we eat only matzah on Pesach?

2)

שֶׁבְּכָל הַלֵּילוֹת אָנוּ אוֹכְלִין שְׁאָר יְרָקוֹת, הַלַּיְלָה הַזֶּה מָרוֹר?

Sheb'chol haleilot anu ochlin she'or yerakot. Halailah hazeh maror.

On all other nights we eat all kinds of vegetables. Why do we eat bitter herbs, maror, at our Seder?

3)

שֶׁבְּכָל הַלֵּילוֹת אֵין אָנוּ מַטְבִּילִין אֲפִלּוּ פַּעַם אֶחָת, הַלַּיְלָה הַזֶּה שְׁתֵּי פְעָמִים?

Sheb'chol haleilot ein anu matbilin afilu pa'am echat. Halailah hazeh sh'tay p'amim.

On all other nights we don't dip food. Tonight, we dip parsley in salt water and bitter herbs in charoset. Why do we dip twice?

4)

שֶׁבְּכָל הַלֵּילוֹת אָנוּ אוֹכְלִין בֵּין יוֹשְׁבִין וּבֵין מְסֻבִּין, הַלַּיְלָה הַזֶּה כֻּלָּנוּ מְסֻבִּין?

Sheb'chol haleilot anu ochlin bein yoshvin u'vein m'subin. Halailah hazeh kulanu m'subin.

On all other nights we eat sitting up straight. Why do we lean on a pillow tonight?

We've already read the story of Pesach, so we should know the answers to these questions!

1) Why Matzah on Pesach?

Matzah reminds us of the hurried escape from Egypt. When the Jews left, there was no time for bread to rise, so they carried raw dough on their backs. The sun worked its magic, turning it into hard crackers - matzah!

2) Why Bitter Herbs?

Bitter herbs, or maror, take us back to the tough times in Egypt. They remind us of how Pharaoh treated the Jewish people bitterly, making them work as slaves.

3) Why Dip Twice?

Dipping bitter herbs in charoset tells the story of hard work in Egypt. Charoset, with apples, wine, and nuts, resembles the clay used for Pharaoh's palaces. We also dip parsley in saltwater – parsley for spring's new life and saltwater for the tears of the Jewish slaves.

4) Why Lean on a Pillow?

Leaning on a pillow isn't just comfortable; it's a reminder. We were once slaves, but now we're free. So, we lean to celebrate our newfound freedom at the Seder!

As we eat the food on the Seder table, we recall the story of Passover.

MATZAH

Matzah reminds us of the Jewish people's hurried flight from slavery in Egypt. We uncover the matzah and break the middle piece, putting half of it away for later. This piece is called the afikoman. We hide it in a safe place so we can find it after the meal.

Each person gets two small pieces of matzah and we say two blessings before eating the matzah.

בָּרוּךְ אַתָה יְיָ אֱלֹהֵינוּ מֶלֶךְ הָעוֹלָם, הַמּוֹצִיא לֶחֶם מִן הָאָרֶץ.

Baruch Atah Adonai Eloheinu Melech ha'olam, hamotzi lechem min ha'aretz.

בָּרוּךְ אַתָה יְיָ אֱלֹהֵינוּ מֶלֶךְ הָעוֹלָם, אֲשֶׁר קִדְּשָׁנוּ בְּמִצְוֹתָיו וְצִוָנוּ עַל אֲכִילַת מַצָּה.

Baruch Atah Adonai Eloheinu Melech ha'olam asher kid'shanu b'mitzvotav v'tzivanu al achilat matzah.

Thank You, God, for the blessing of bread, and for the special matzah eat eat on Pesach.

PARSLEY

Parsley recalls the spring when God brought the Jewish people out of slavery. We dip the parsley in salt water and say a blessing before eating it.

בָּרוּךְ אַתָּה יְיָ אֱלֹהֵינוּ מֶלֶךְ הָעוֹלָם, בּוֹרֵא פְּרִי הָאֲדָמָה.

Baruch Atah Adonai Eloheinu Melech ha'olam, borei p'ri ha'adamah.

Thank You, God, for the vegetables that grow in the ground.

MAROR

Maror reminds us of the bitterness of slavery. We dip the maror in charoset and recite a blessing before eating it.

בָּרוּךְ אַתָּה יְיָ אֱלֹהֵינוּ מֶלֶךְ הָעוֹלָם, אֲשֶׁר קִדְּשָׁנוּ בְּמִצְוֹתָיו וְצִוָּנוּ עַל אֲכִילַת מָרוֹר.

Baruch Atah Adonai Eloheinu Melech ha'olam asher kid'shanu b'mitzvotav v'tzivanu al achilat maror.

Thank You, God, for maror.

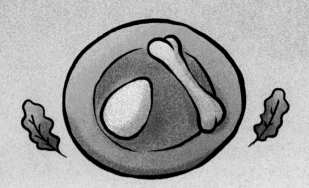

THE EGG AND THE BONE

On the Passover plate, we have two more special symbols.
The egg reminds us of spring when the Jews were freed from
Egypt.
The bone brings us back to the first Passover
celebration, where people roasted a lamb and ate it with
matzah.

CUP OF ELIJAH

The special cup on the table is known as the Cup of Elijah. Legend has it that Elijah, a great teacher from the past, stops by every Seder to wish us a year of peace and freedom. We open the door and invite Elijah inside. Keep an eye on his cup – who knows, the wine might just disappear!

Now is the time for our Seder meal.

B'teavon!

Oh, and whoever finds the afikoman first gets a reward!

We finish our Seder meal with a blessing.

בָּרוּךְ אַתָּה יְיָ הַזָּן אֶת הַכֹּל.

Baruch Atah Adonai hazan et hakol.

Thank You, God, for the food we have eaten.
We end with a song of thanks to God, for taking us out of
slavery to freedom, for giving us the Torah, and bringing us to
the land of Israel.

HAPPY
PASSOVER!

Made in the USA
Las Vegas, NV
20 April 2024

88918867R00019